THAT VITILIGO GUY

Copyright © 2020 James Mcleod Jr. and Jenifer C. Orefice.
Illustrations by Taylor Flagler.

ISBN: 978-0-578-78304-8

All rights reserved. No part of this book may be reproduced, stored, or transmitted by any means—whether auditory, graphic, mechanical, or electronic—without written permission of both publisher and author, except in the case of brief excerpts used in critical articles and reviews. Unauthorized reproduction of any part of this work is illegal and is punishable by law.

Hi, my name is James! It's nice to meet you!

I used to not like it that I look different than other kids.

I used to have a lot of bad days, but now I have good days!

Being different is cool! Being different
is one of my superpowers!

Once I realized I could be my own superhero,
I realized I have SO MANY superpowers!

Do you have superpowers too?
I bet you do and you don't even know it!

I'm going to share some of mine with you,
and I hope you discover yours!!!

Today, my superpower is bravery.

Today, my superpower is love.

Today, my superpower is self-acceptance.

Today, my superpower is leadership.

I don't know everything, and that's okay! I am ready to learn.

Today, my superpower is being silly.

There is no one in the world
like me, and I am awesome!

I know you have what it takes to be your own Superhero too!!!

There are so many things to love about YOU!

Made in the USA
Middletown, DE
18 July 2024

57452599R00018